First Graphics

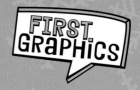

Seasons

Winter Is Wonderful

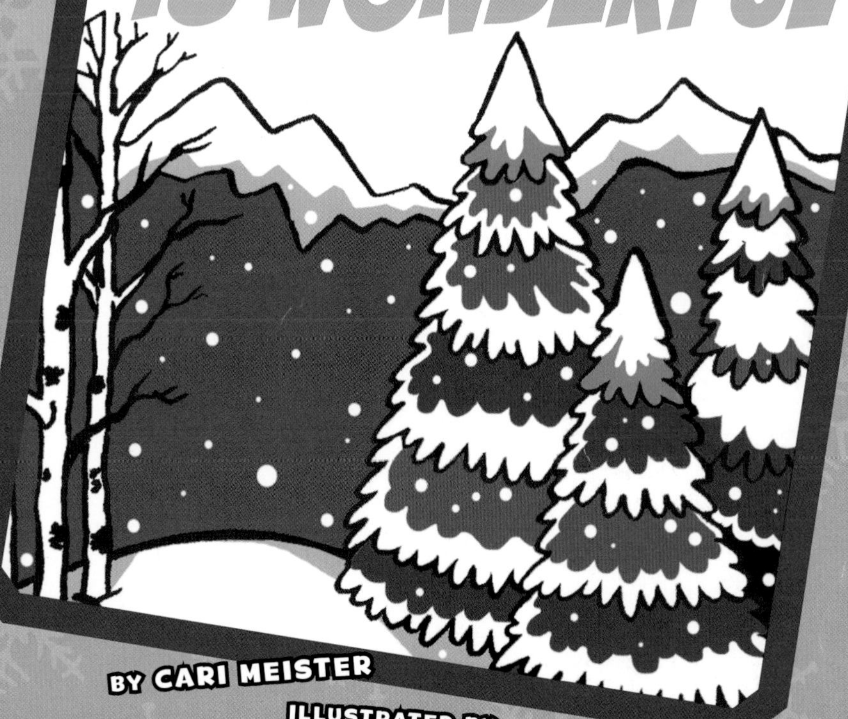

By Cari Meister

Illustrated by Jim Lingenfelter

CAPSTONE PRESS
a capstone imprint

First Graphics are published by Capstone Press,
151 Good Counsel Drive, P.O. Box 669, Mankato, Minnesota 56002.
www.capstonepub.com

Printed in the United States of America in Stevens Point, Wisconsin.

032010
005741WZF10

Books published by Capstone Press are manufactured with paper containing at least 10 percent post-consumer waste.

Library of Congress Cataloging-in-Publication Data

Meister, Cari.
Winter is wonderful / by Cari Meister ; illustrated by Jim Lingenfelter.
p. cm. — (First graphics. Seasons.)
Includes index.
ISBN 978-1-4296-4732-8 (library binding)
ISBN 978-1-4296-5624-5 (paperback)
1. Winter—Juvenile literature. I. Title. II. Series.
QB637.8.M45 2011 2010000041
508.2—dc22

Editor: **Shelly Lyons**
Designer: **Alison Thiele**
Art Director: **Nathan Gassman**
Production Specialist: **Laura Manthe**

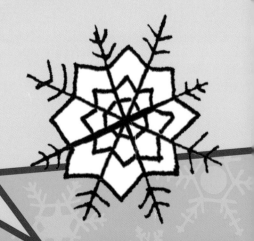

TABLE OF CONTENTS

What Is Winter?

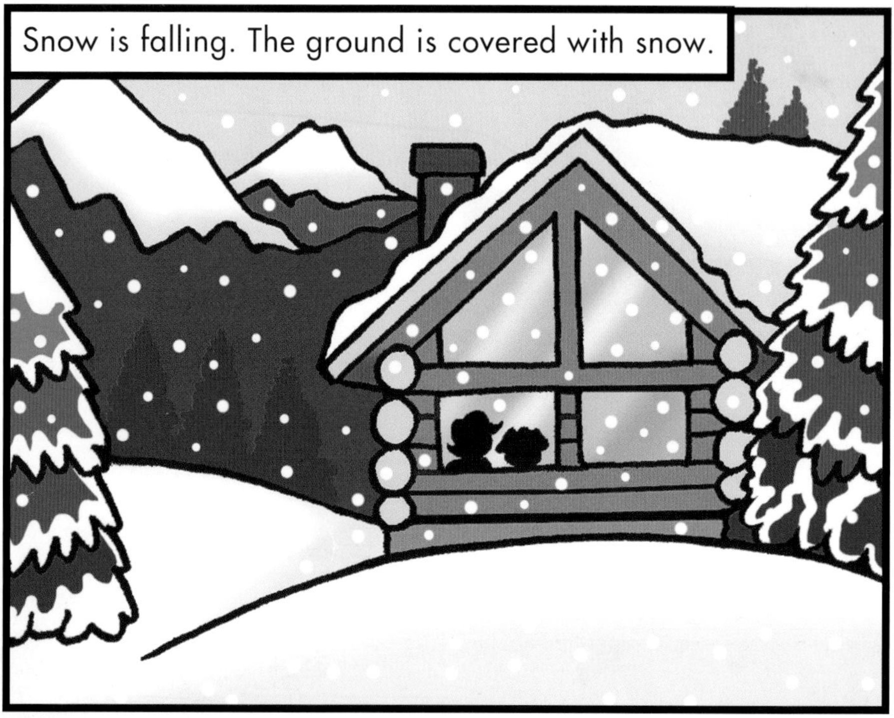
Snow is falling. The ground is covered with snow.

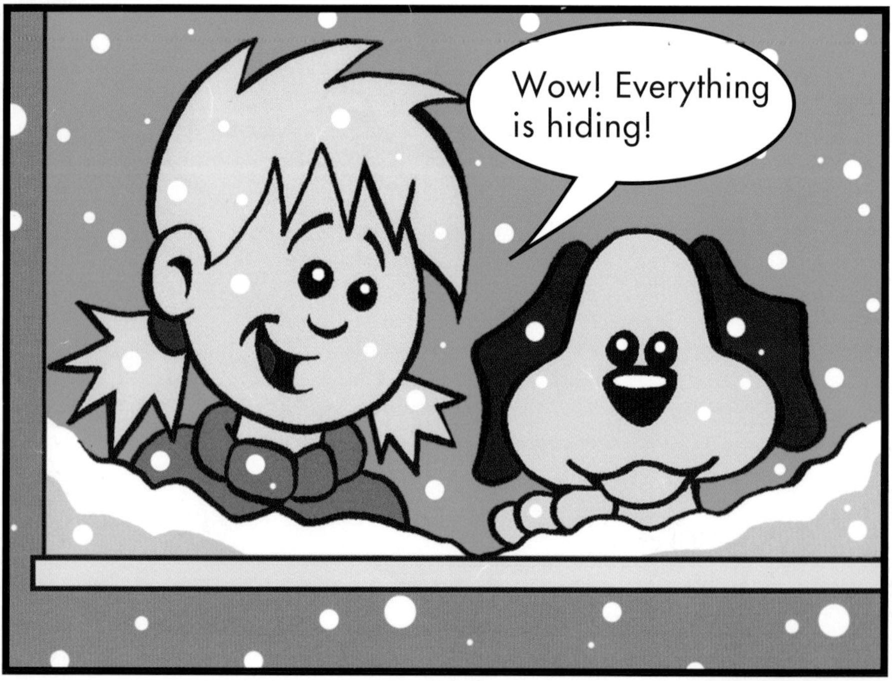
Wow! Everything is hiding!

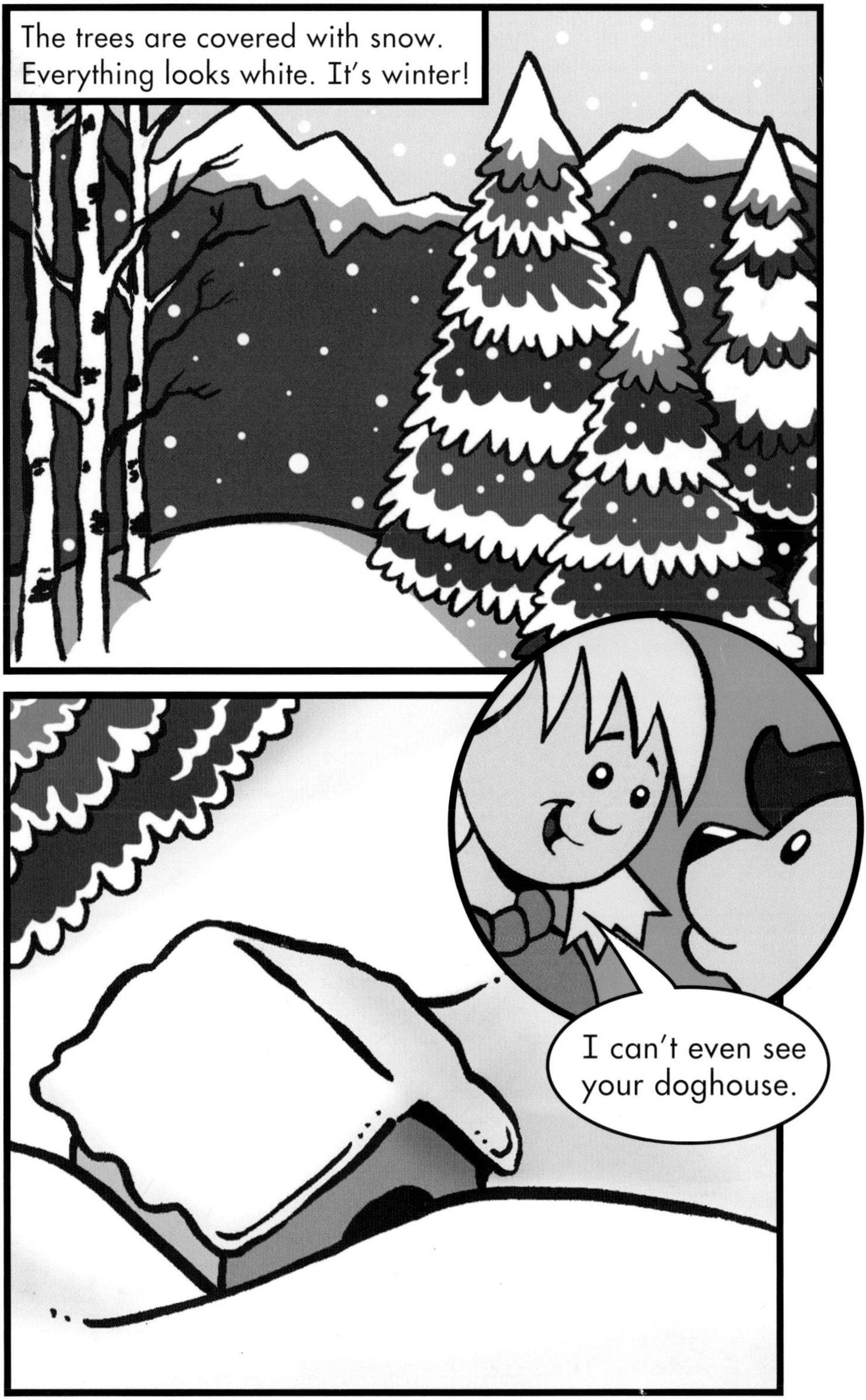
The trees are covered with snow. Everything looks white. It's winter!
I can't even see your doghouse.

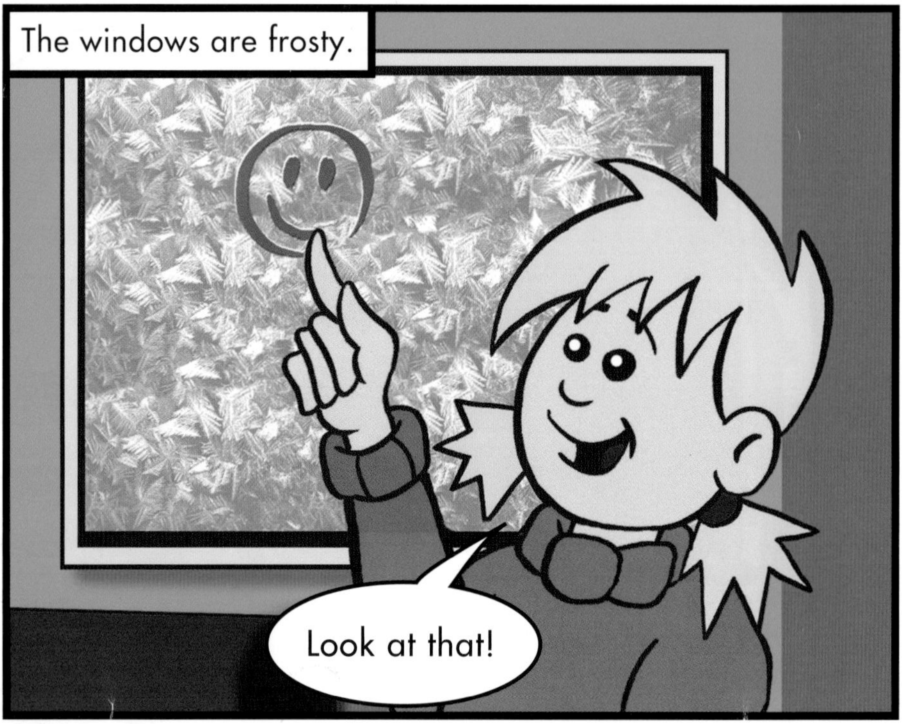
The windows are frosty.
Look at that!

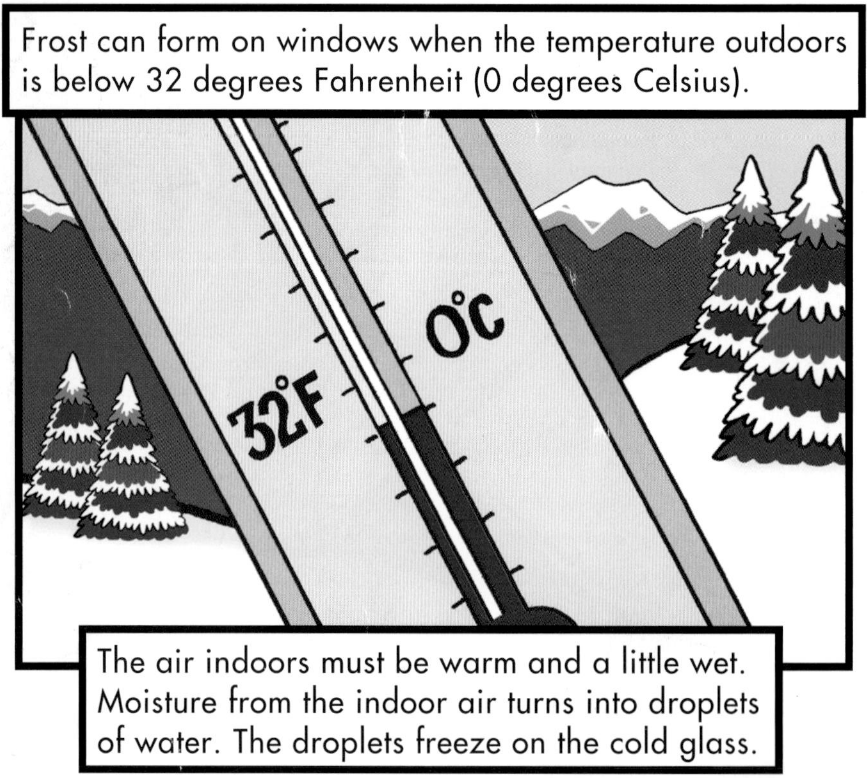
Frost can form on windows when the temperature outdoors is below 32 degrees Fahrenheit (0 degrees Celsius).
32°F
0°C
The air indoors must be warm and a little wet. Moisture from the indoor air turns into droplets of water. The droplets freeze on the cold glass.

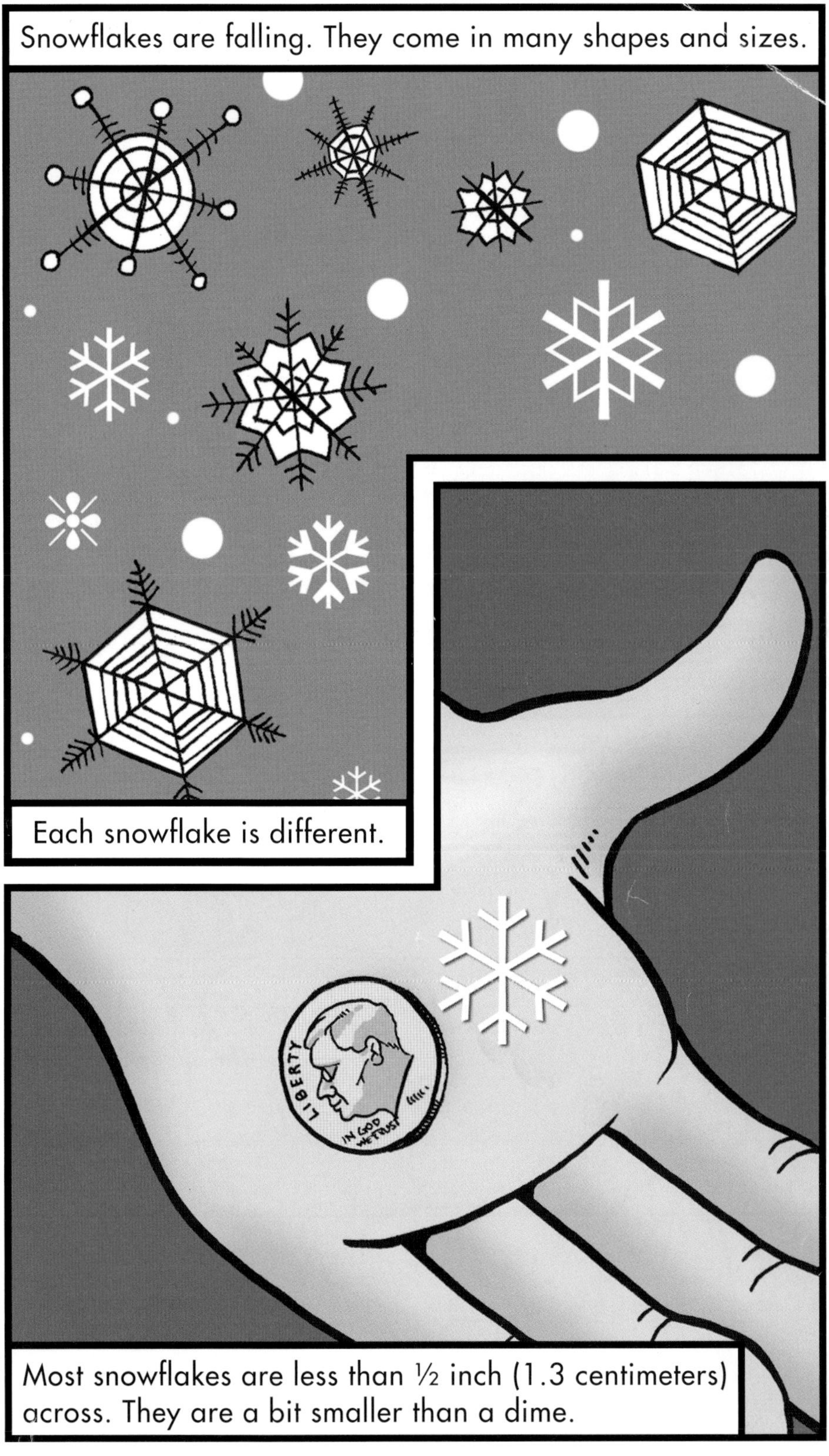
Snowflakes are falling. They come in many shapes and sizes.
Each snowflake is different.
LIBERTY
IN GOD WE TRUST
Most snowflakes are less than ½ inch (1.3 centimeters) across. They are a bit smaller than a dime.

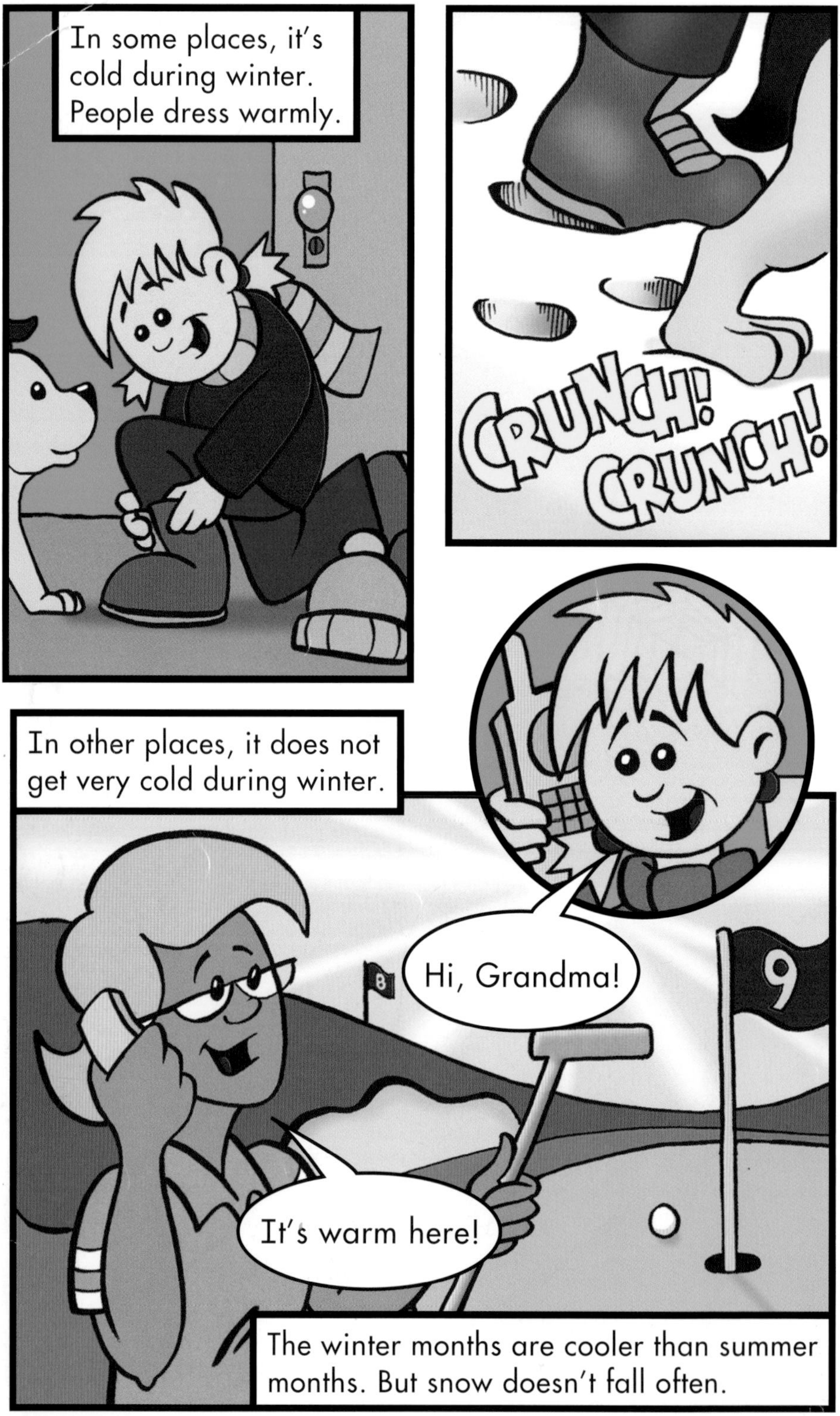
In some places, it's cold during winter. People dress warmly.
CRUNCH! CRUNCH!
In other places, it does not get very cold during winter.
Hi, Grandma!
It's warm here!
The winter months are cooler than summer months. But snow doesn't fall often.

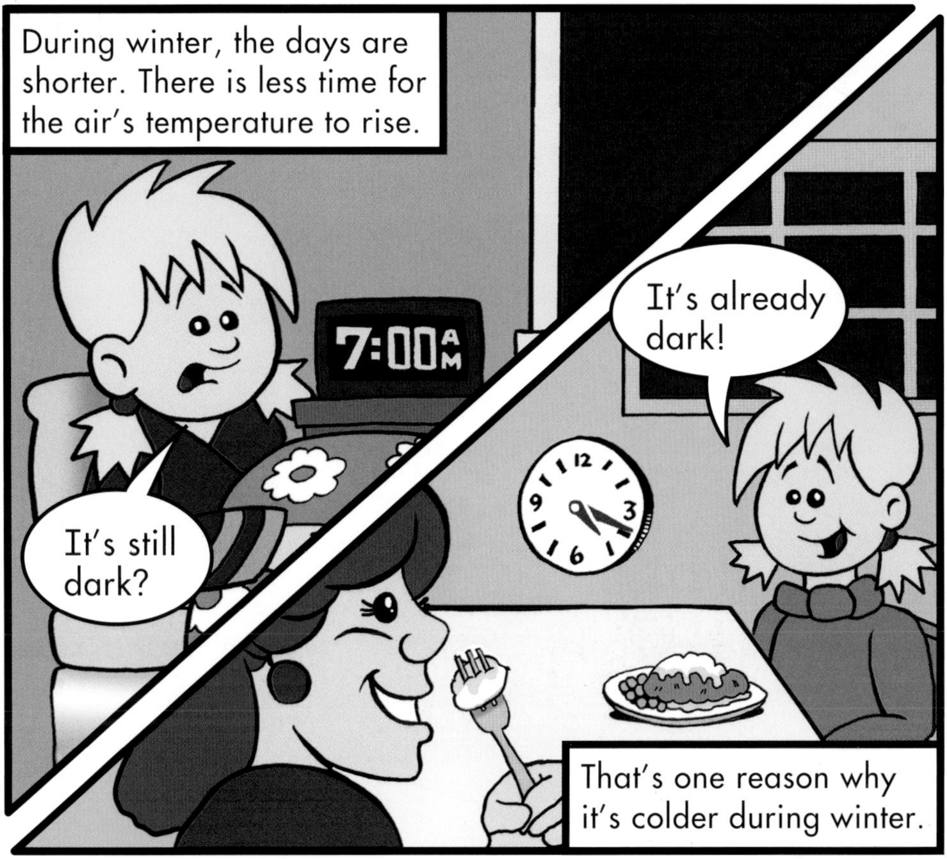
During winter, the days are shorter. There is less time for the air's temperature to rise.
It's still dark?
7:00 AM
It's already dark!
That's one reason why it's colder during winter.

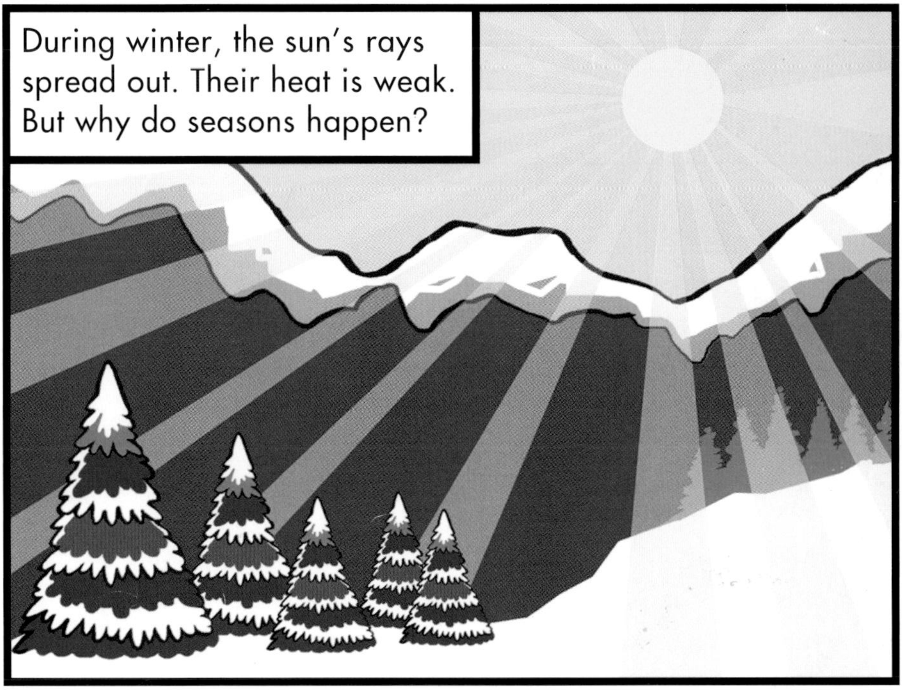
During winter, the sun's rays spread out. Their heat is weak. But why do seasons happen?

Earth is always tilted at the same angle. It moves around the sun once in a year. As Earth moves, it spins on its axis.

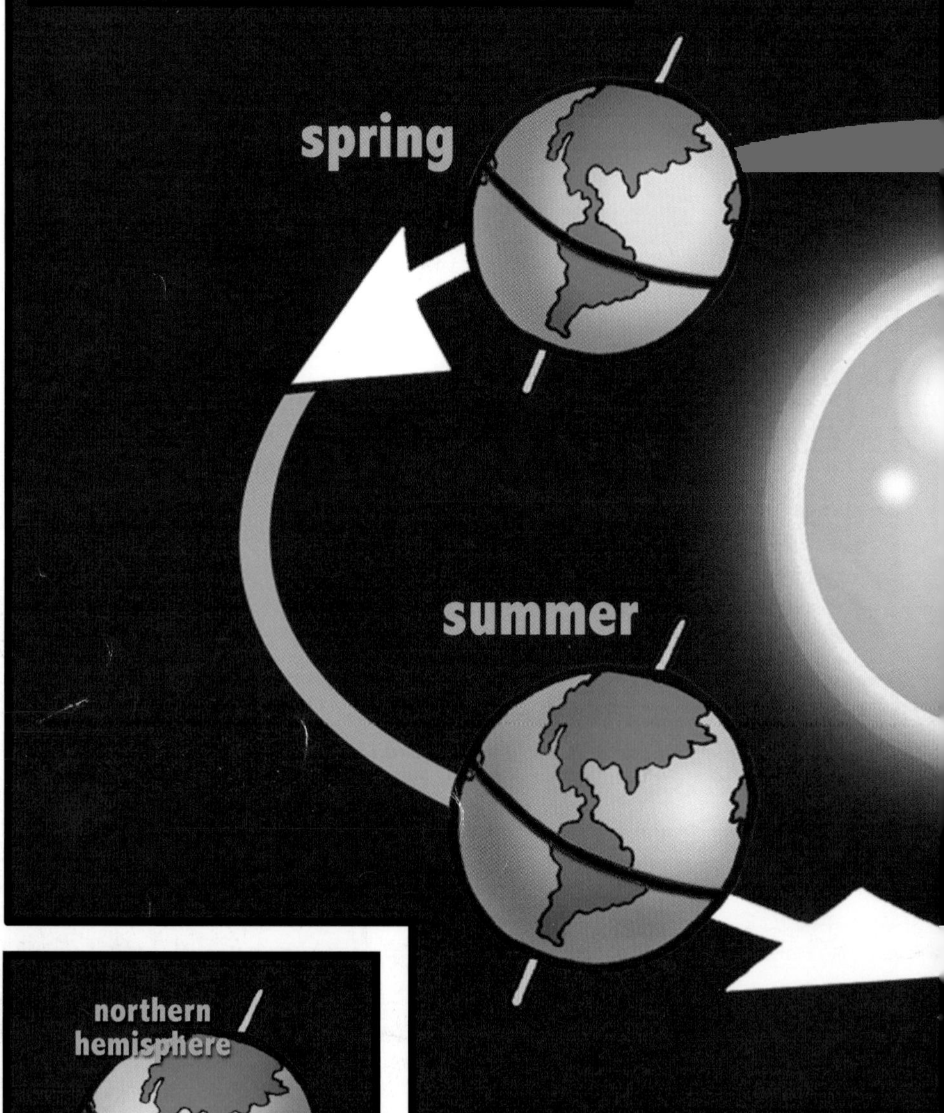
spring
summer

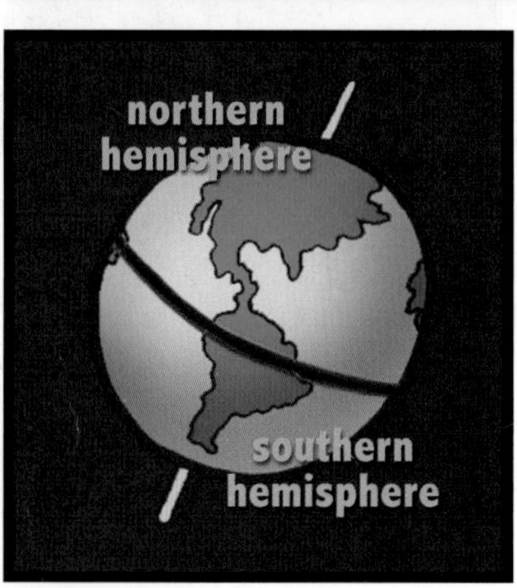
northern hemisphere
southern hemisphere

Earth has a northern and a southern hemisphere.

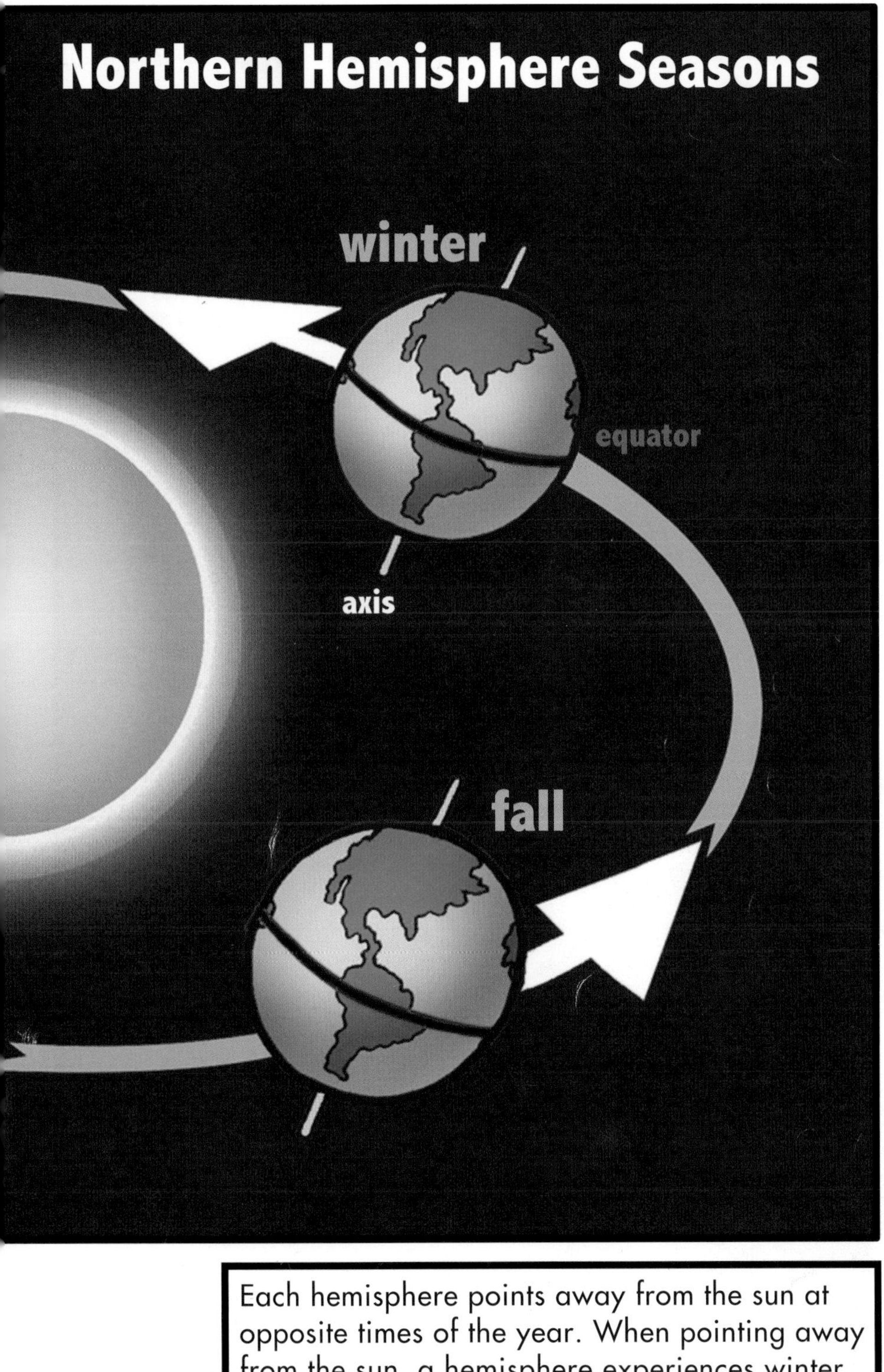
Northern Hemisphere Seasons
winter
equator
axis
fall

Each hemisphere points away from the sun at opposite times of the year. When pointing away from the sun, a hemisphere experiences winter.

Animals During Winter

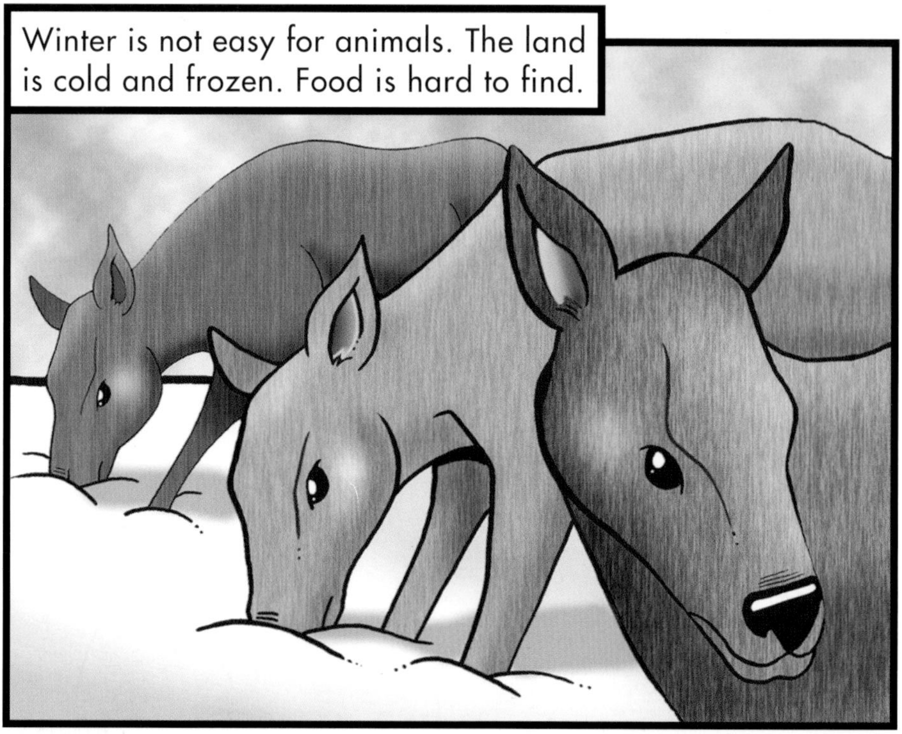
Winter is not easy for animals. The land is cold and frozen. Food is hard to find.

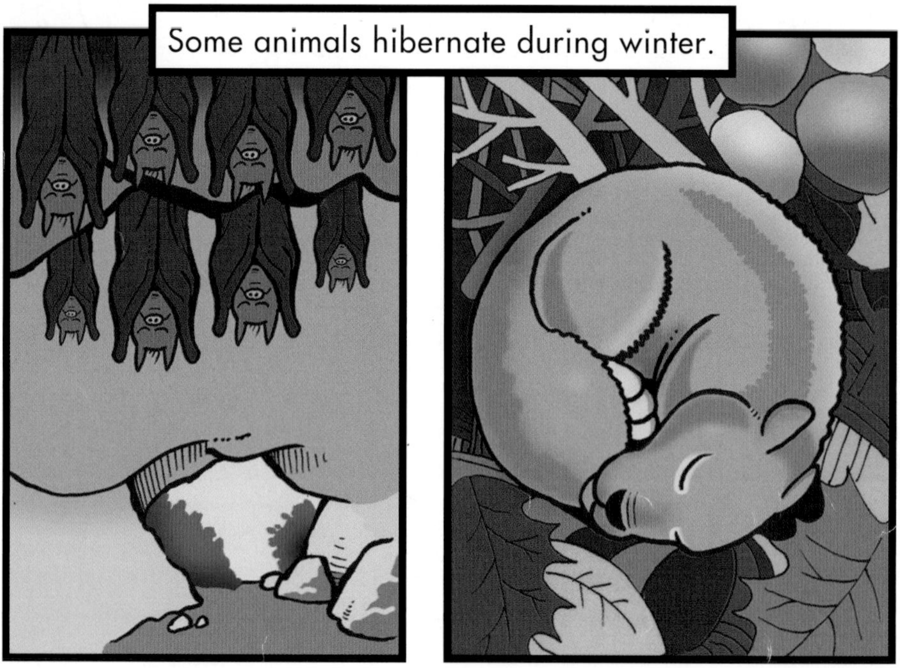
Some animals hibernate during winter.

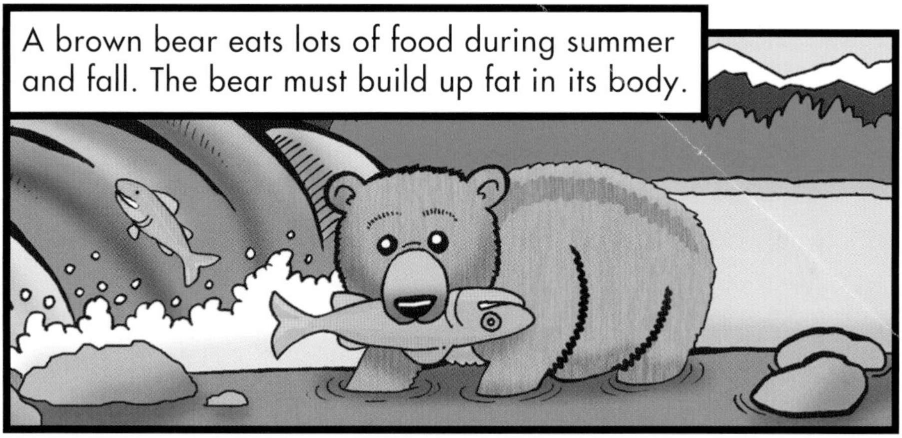
A brown bear eats lots of food during summer and fall. The bear must build up fat in its body.

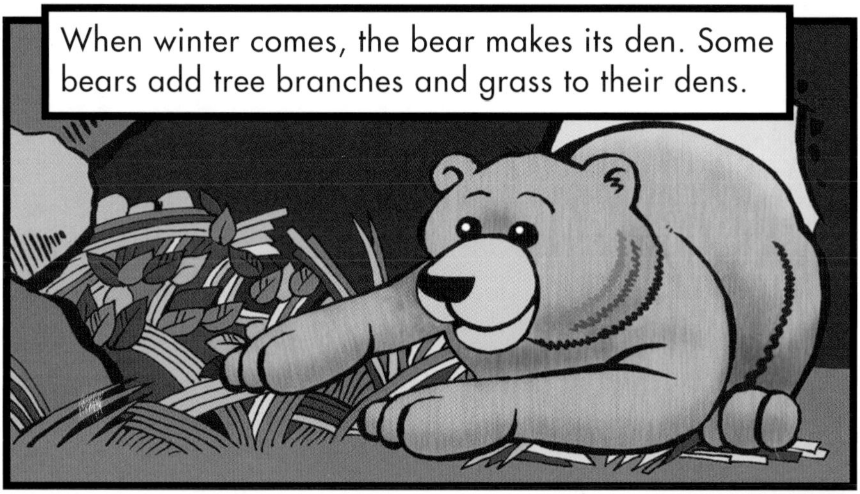
When winter comes, the bear makes its den. Some bears add tree branches and grass to their dens.

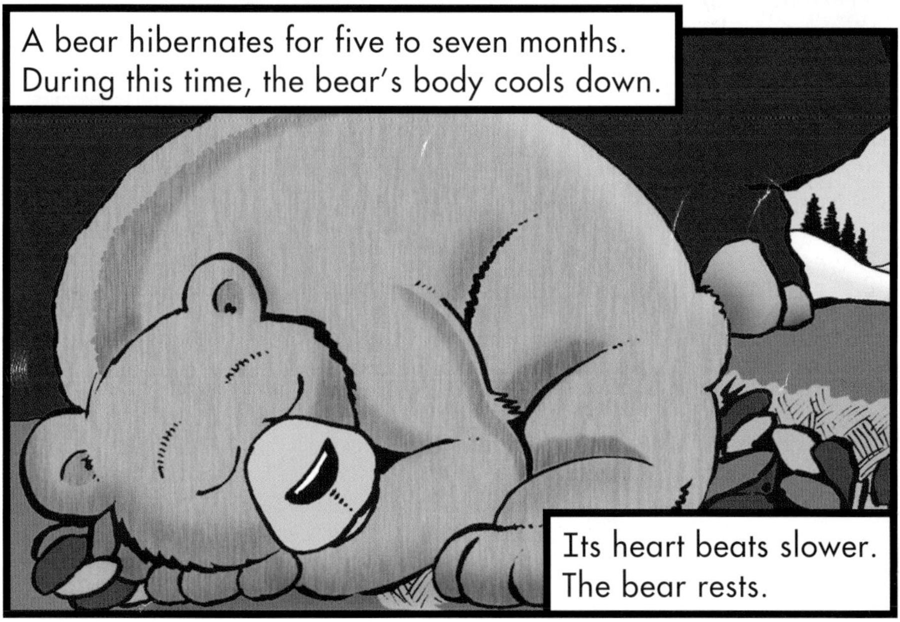
A bear hibernates for five to seven months. During this time, the bear's body cools down.
Its heart beats slower. The bear rests.

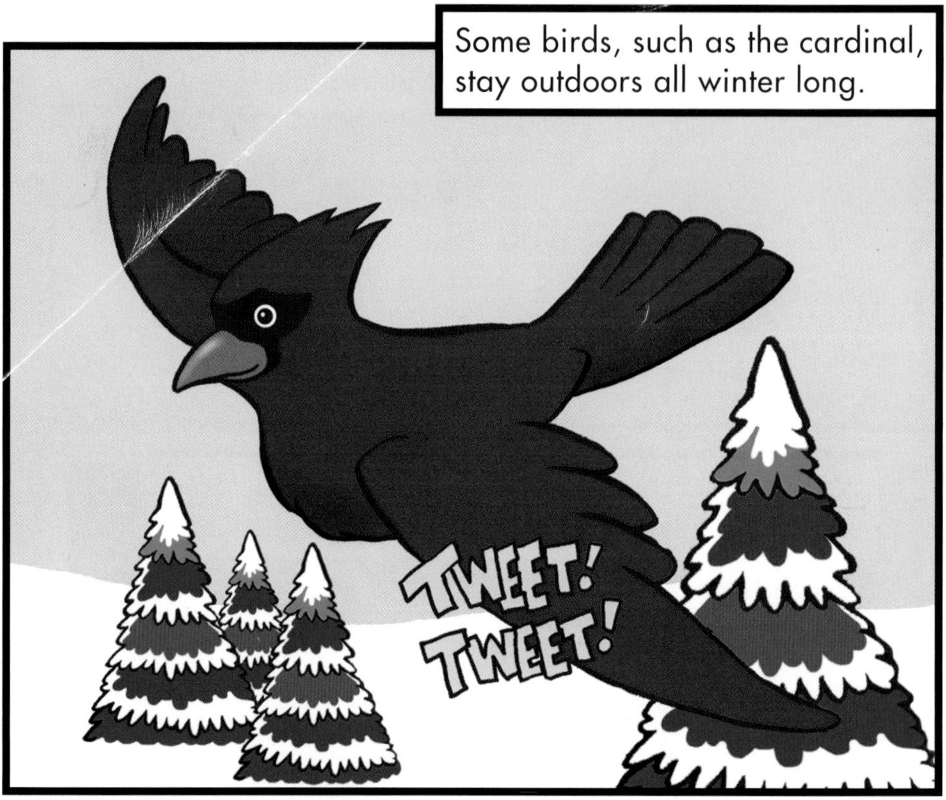
Some birds, such as the cardinal, stay outdoors all winter long.
TWEET! TWEET!

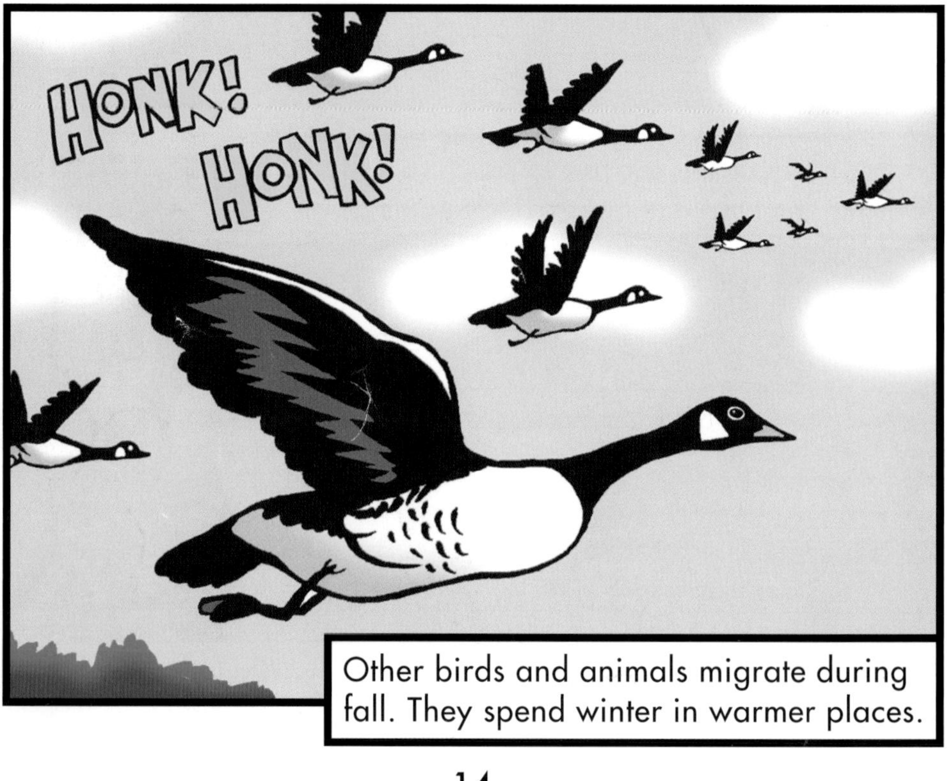
HONK! HONK!
Other birds and animals migrate during fall. They spend winter in warmer places.

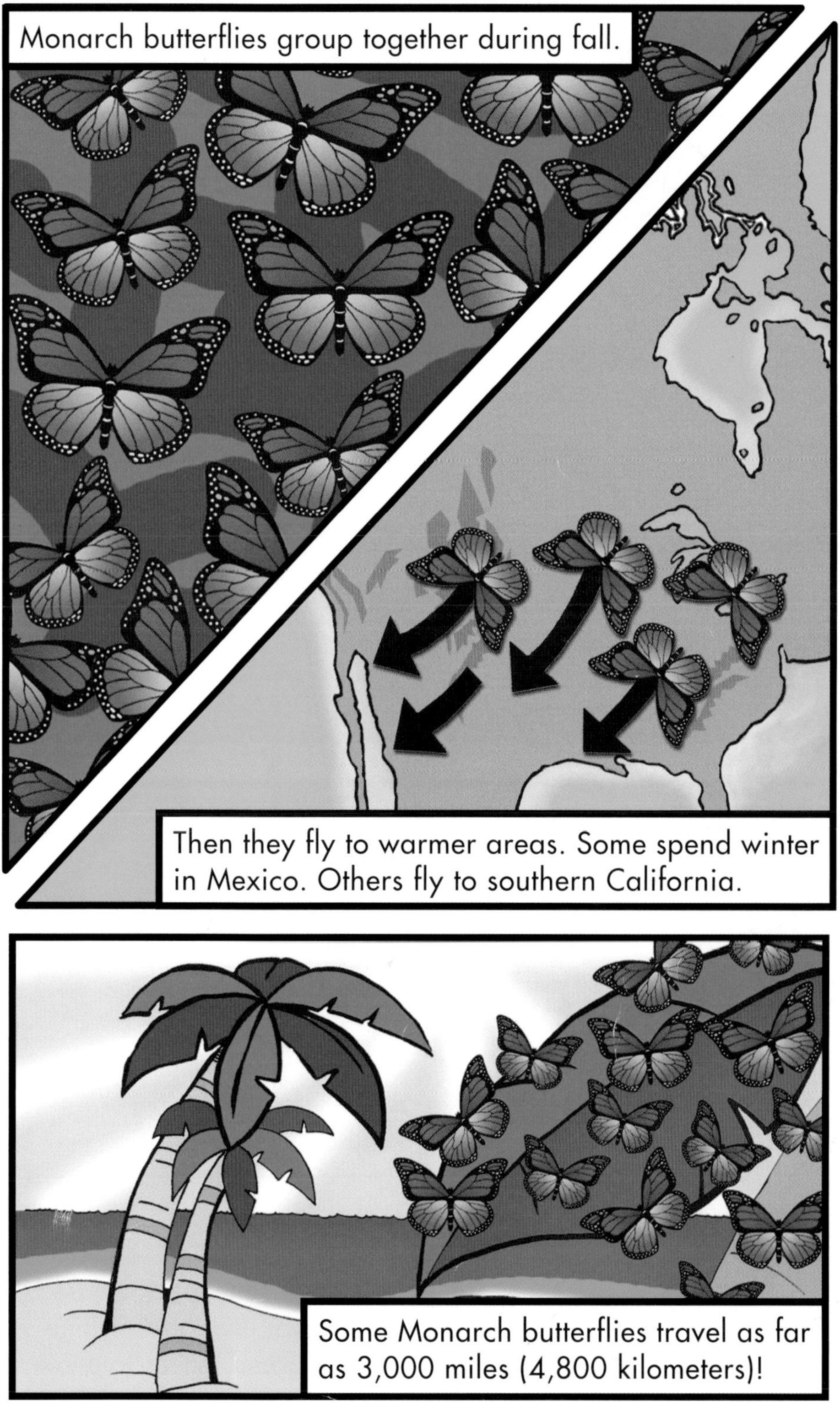
Monarch butterflies group together during fall.
Then they fly to warmer areas. Some spend winter in Mexico. Others fly to southern California.
Some Monarch butterflies travel as far as 3,000 miles (4,800 kilometers)!

Plants and Trees

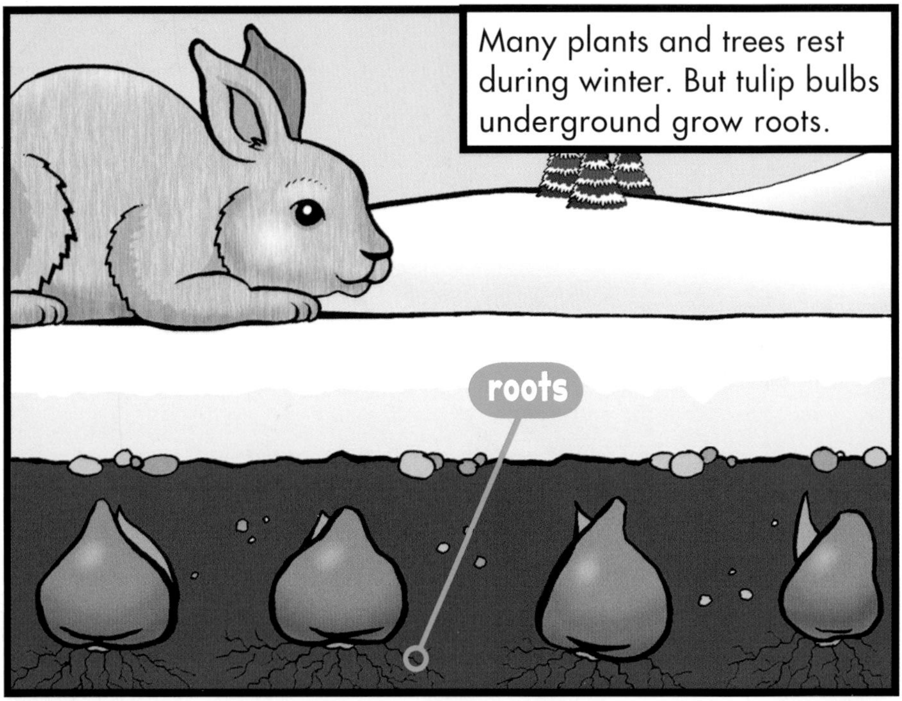

Many plants and trees rest during winter. But tulip bulbs underground grow roots.
roots

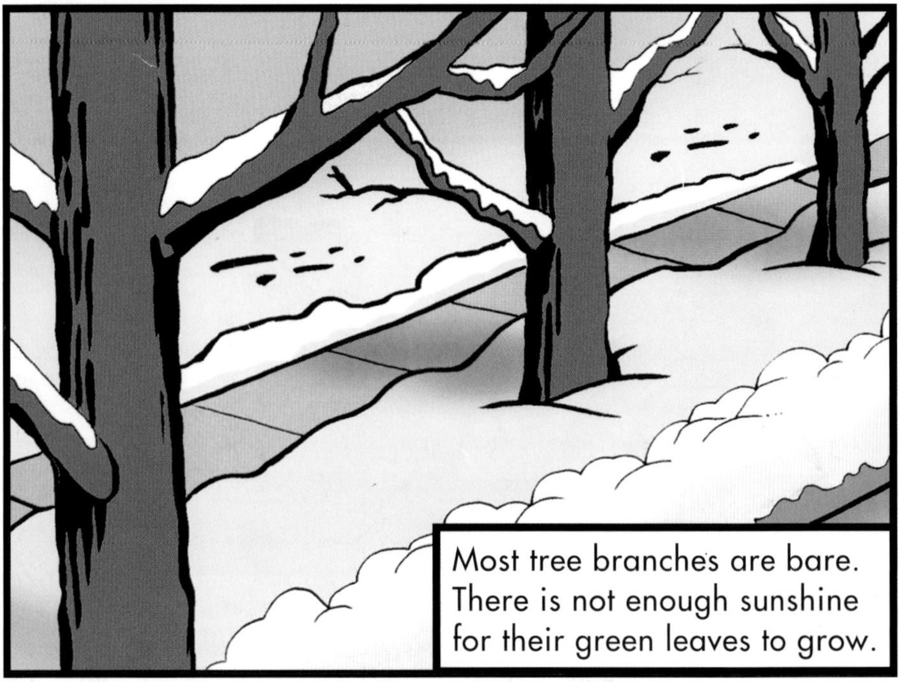

Most tree branches are bare. There is not enough sunshine for their green leaves to grow.

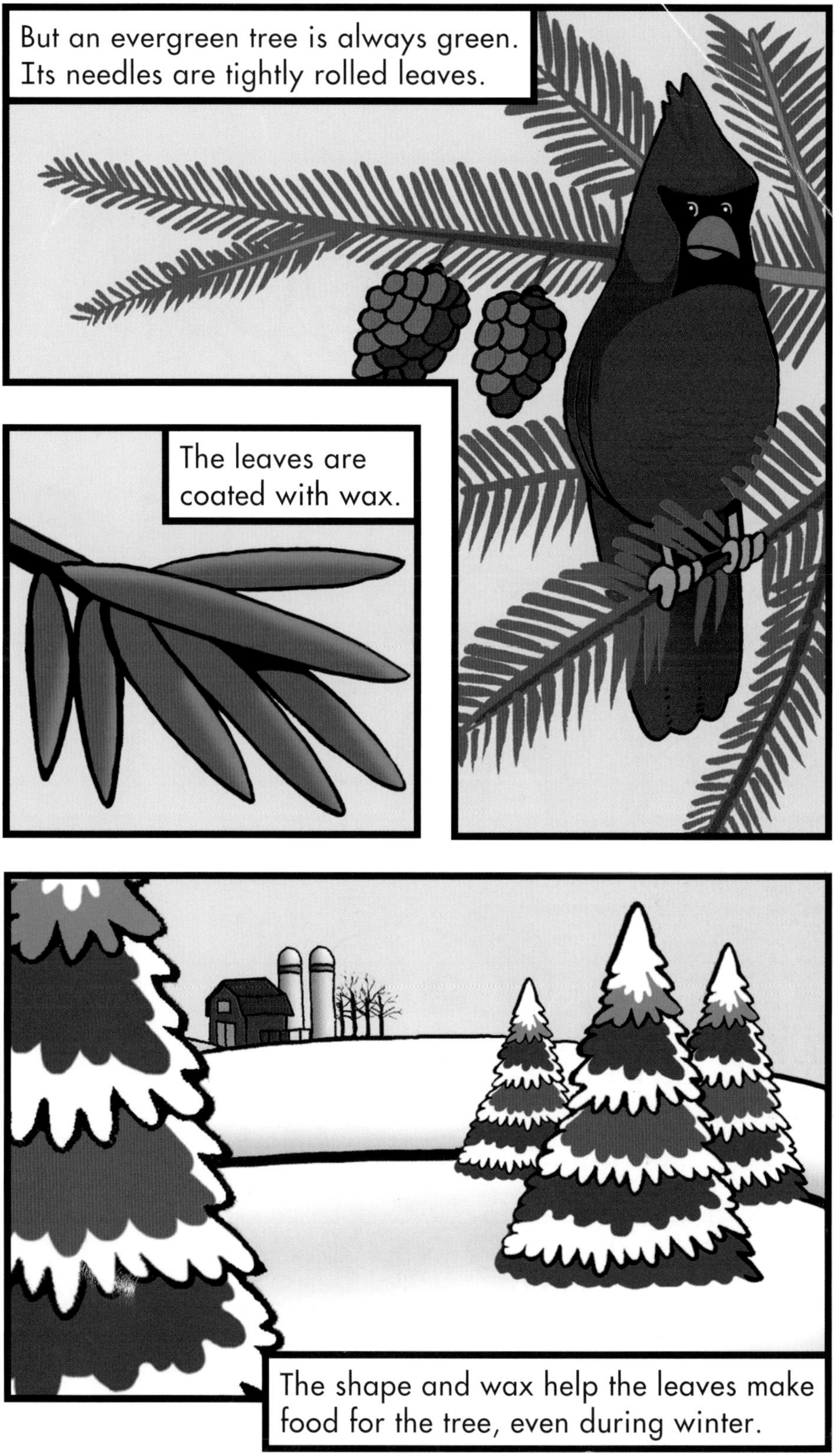
But an evergreen tree is always green. Its needles are tightly rolled leaves.
The leaves are coated with wax.
The shape and wax help the leaves make food for the tree, even during winter.

WINTER FUN

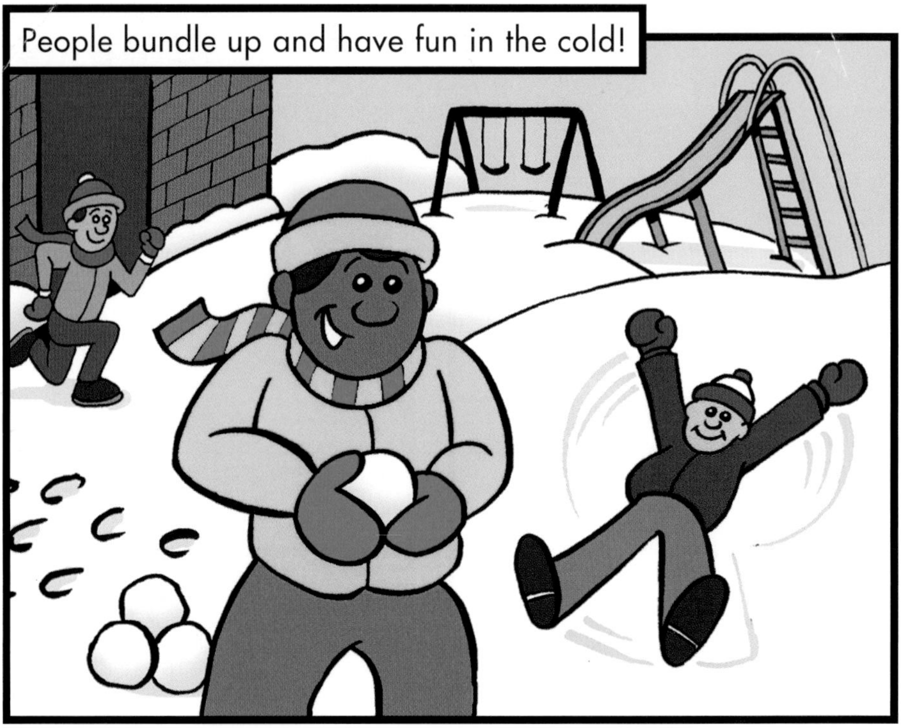

People bundle up and have fun in the cold!

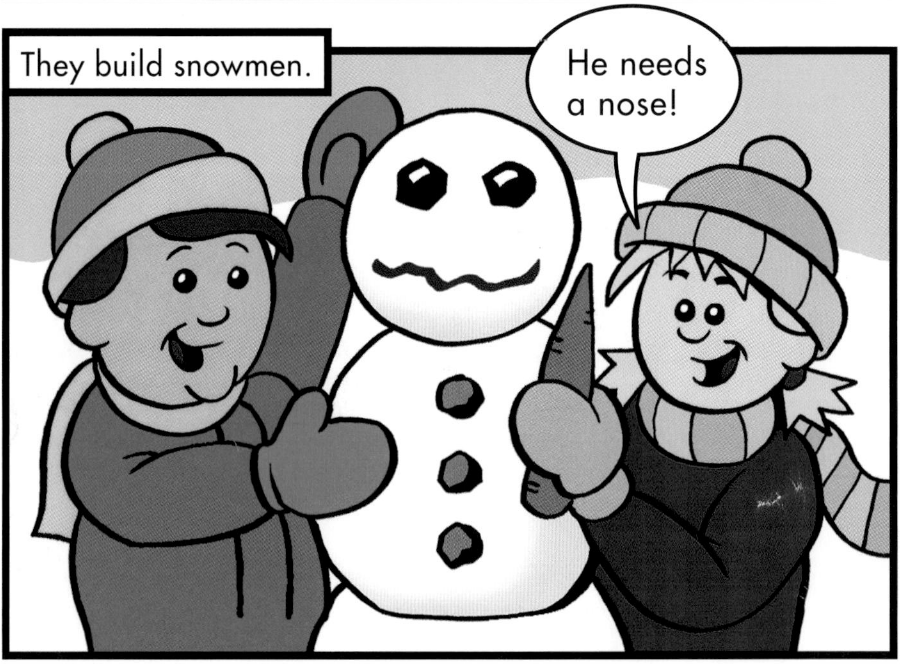

They build snowmen.
He needs a nose!

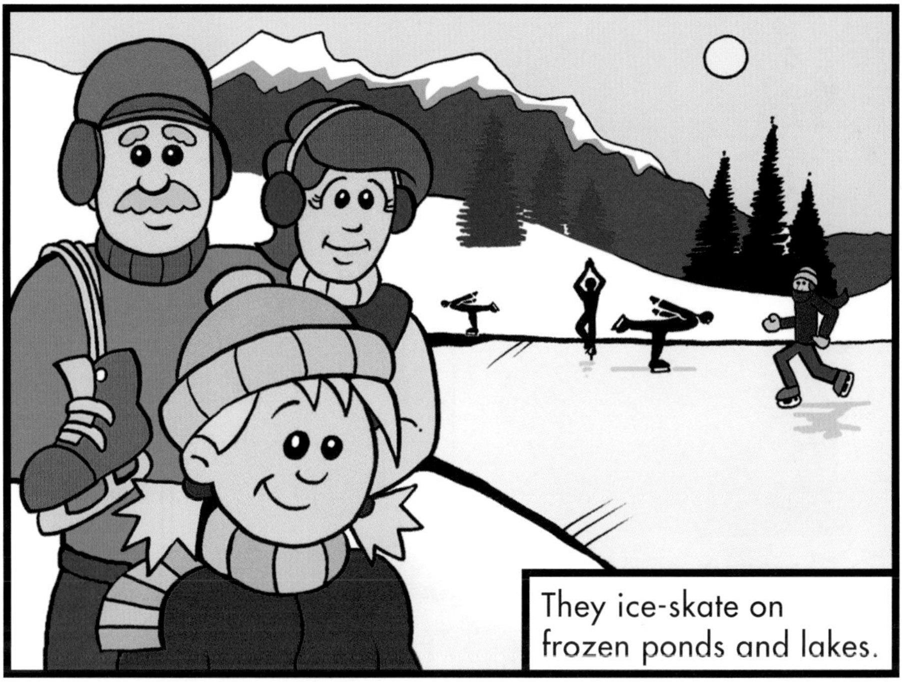
They ice-skate on
frozen ponds and lakes.

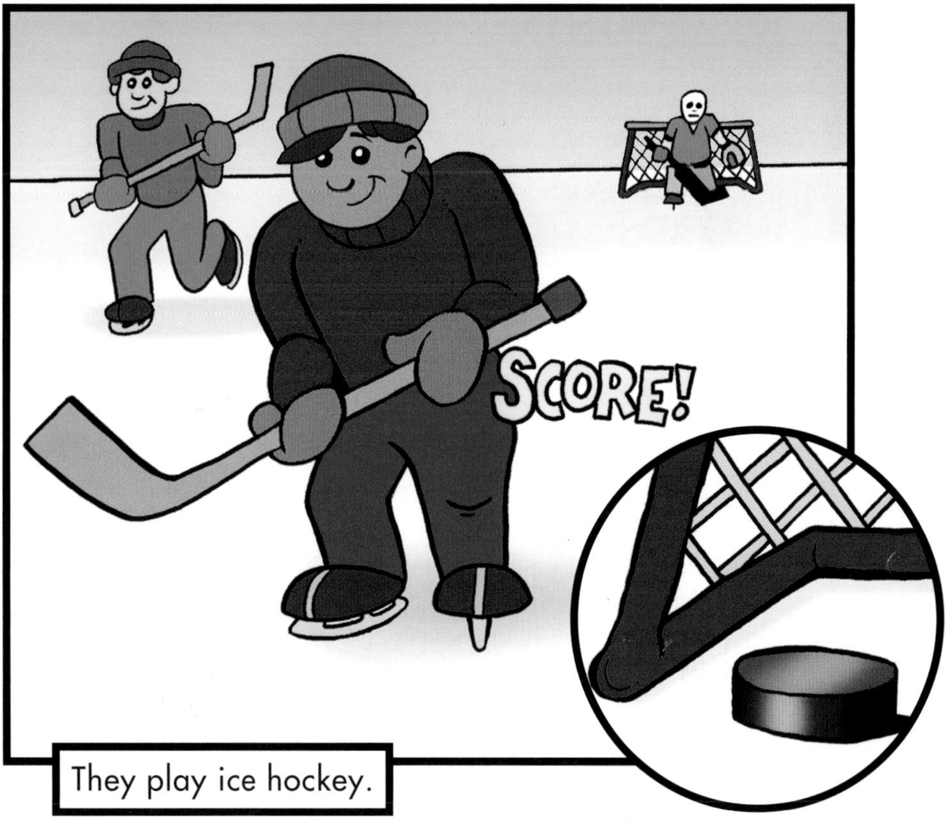
SCORE!
They play ice hockey.

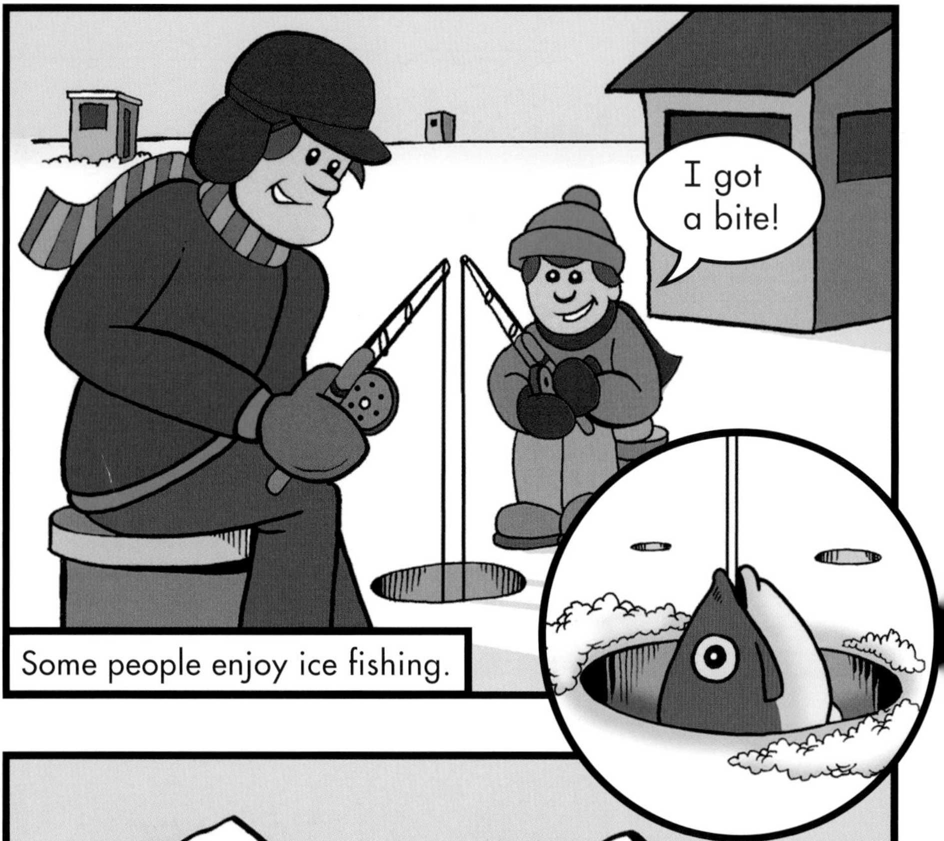
I got a bite!
Some people enjoy ice fishing.

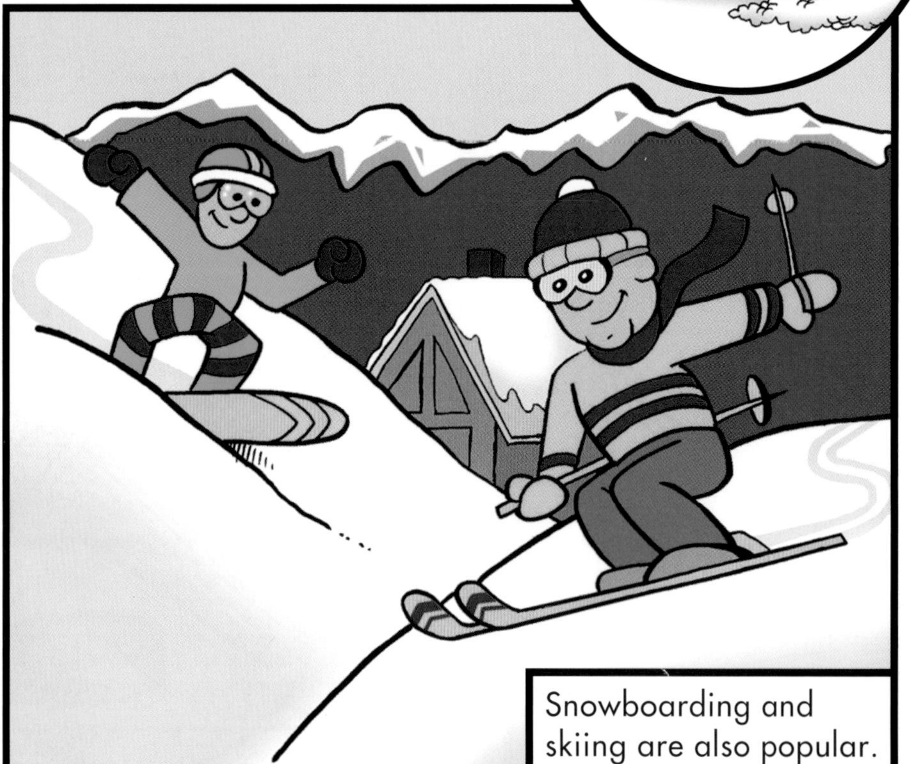
Snowboarding and skiing are also popular.

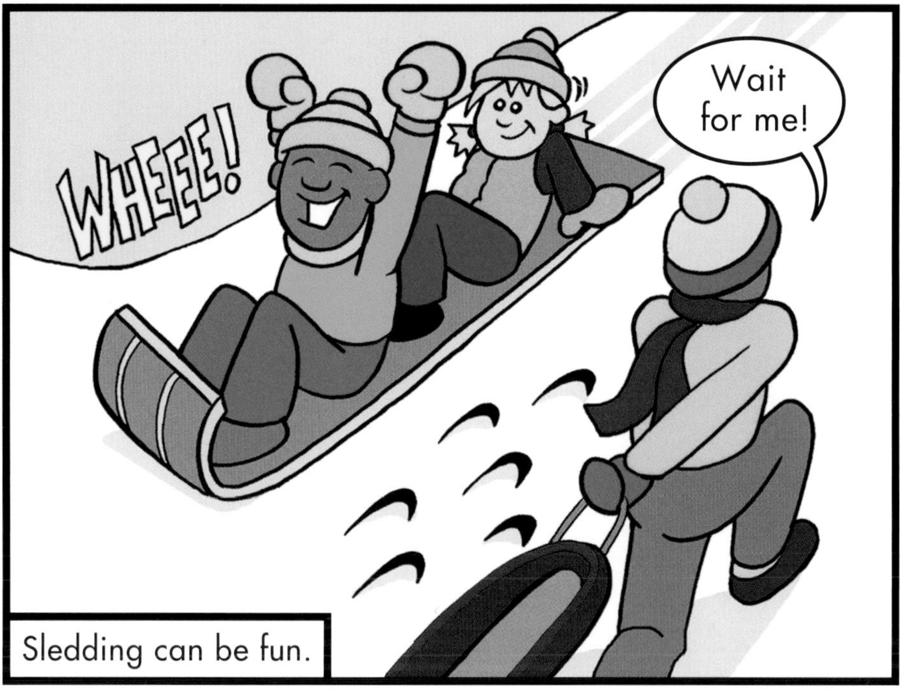
WHEEE!
Wait for me!
Sledding can be fun.

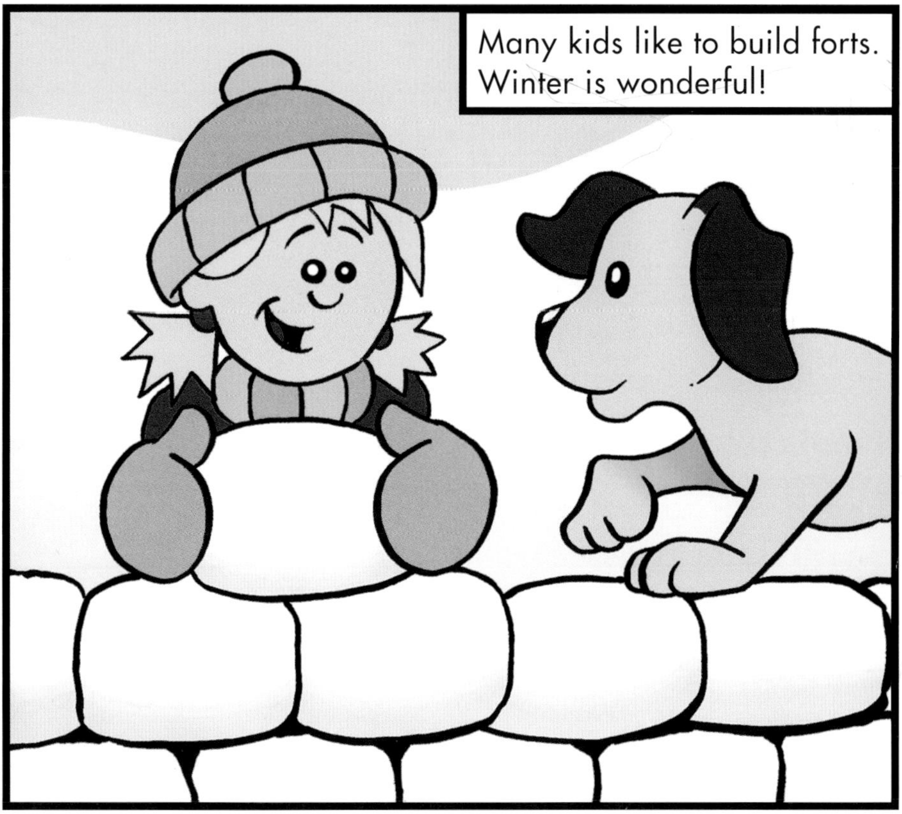
Many kids like to build forts.
Winter is wonderful!

GLOSSARY

angle—the figure formed by two lines or flat surfaces that extend from one point or line

axis—an imaginary line that runs through the middle of Earth from the North Pole to the South Pole

bulb—a round underground part of a plant from which the plant grows

droplet—a small drop of water

equator—an imaginary line around the middle of Earth; areas near the equator are usually warm and wet

evergreen—a tree that stays green all year

hemisphere—one half of Earth

hibernate—to deeply sleep or rest quietly during winter

migrate—to regularly move from place to place to find food or shelter

moisture—water in the air

root—a part of the plant that is underground; roots bring water to the plant

temperature—how hot or cold something is

READ MORE

Latta, Sara L. *What Happens in Winter?* I Like the Seasons! Berkeley Heights, N.J.: Enslow Publishers, 2006.

Salas, Laura Purdie. *Do Polar Bears Snooze in Hollow Trees?: A Book About Animal Hibernation.* Animals All Around. Minneapolis: Picture Window Books, 2007.

Stewart, Melissa. *Why Do the Seasons Change?* Tell Me Why, Tell Me How. New York: Marshall Cavendish Benchmark, 2007.

INTERNET SITES

FactHound offers a safe, fun way to find Internet sites related to this book. All of the sites on FactHound have been researched by our staff.

Here's all you do:

Visit *www.facthound.com*

Type in this code: 9781429647328

INDEX

SEASONS

TITLES IN THIS SET:

FALL IS FUN

SPRING IS SPECIAL

SUMMER IS SUPER

WINTER IS WONDERFUL

FIRST GRAPHICS

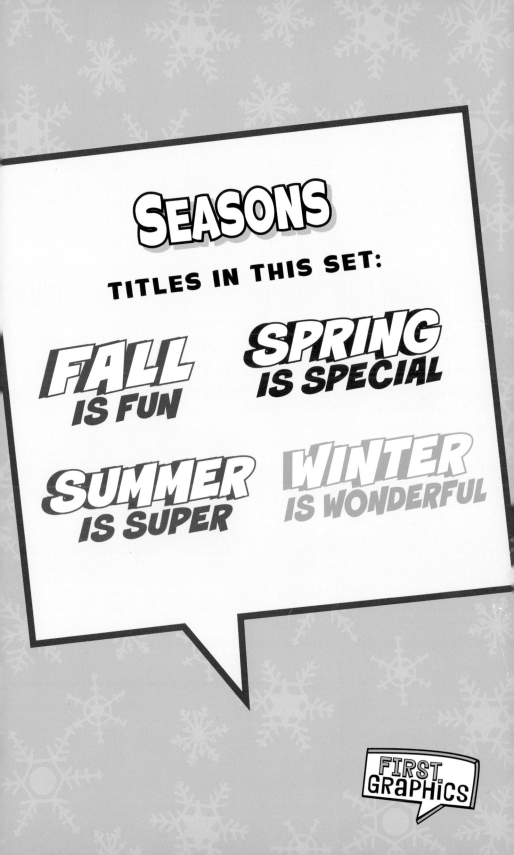